Facts About the Chirping Parakeet

By Lisa Strattin

© 2016 Lisa Strattin

Facts for Kids Picture Books by Lisa Strattin

Canada Lynx, Vol 114

Blue Tarantula, Vol 115

Giant Tarantula, Vol 116

Common Nighthawk, Vol 117

Nile Crocodile, Vol 118

Nilgai, Vol 119

North American Porcupine, Vol 120

Numbat, Vol 121

Nuthatch, Vol 122

Nyala, Vol 123

Sign Up For New Release Emails Here

http://lisastrattin.com/subscribe-here

Join the KidCrafts Monthly Program Here

http://KidCraftsByLisa.com

All information in this book has been carefully researched and checked for factual accuracy. However, the author and publisher makes no warranty, express or implied, that the information contained herein is appropriate for every individual, situation or purpose and assume no responsibility for errors or omissions. The reader assumes the risk and full responsibility for all actions, and the author will not be held responsible for any loss or damage, whether consequential, incidental, special or otherwise, that may result from the information presented in this book.

I have relied on my own observations as well as many different sources for this book and I have done my best to check facts and give credit where it is due. In the event that any material is used without proper permission, please contact me so that the oversight can be corrected.

Table of Contents

INTRODUCTION

The word "parakeet" does not refer to a specific kind of bird. Rather, it refers to several groups of birds with similar characteristics. All parakeets are parrots—though not all parrots are parakeets. "Parakeet" means "long tail," and this feature perhaps more than any other distinguishes a parakeet from other types of parrots.

These birds can be found around the world, including the Americas, Africa, Asia, and Australia. It is said that the Australian and American parakeets have the best colors—though that opinion may depend on who is looking at the bird.

CHARACTERISTICS

Parakeets are as well known for their bright plumage as for being intelligent, social birds. In the wild, they flock sometimes in large numbers, and in captivity they can be affectionate with people as well as other household pets.

Perhaps most interestingly, they have the ability to learn to repeat words or sounds that aren't natural to birds—not only can they learn to reproduce words, but they will also repeat the sound of a barking dog, or a hissing cat, or even a squeaking door!

Parakeets use their beaks in the same way we use our hands. Their beaks have a hooked bill and they can use it to help them climb, grab and hold onto objects, or even to dig. Of course, they also use their bill to eat—it helps them break into the tough outer shell of seeds, fruits, and nuts.

APPEARANCE

Parakeets are medium-sized parrots. Their plumage is frequently bright and colorful, including vibrant greens, reds, blues, oranges, and yellows—though this varies depending on the type of bird. All parakeets have tail feathers that taper—or come to a point—and are nearly half the length of their body.

LIFE STAGES

As birds, parakeets start their life as eggs. It takes nearly three weeks for an egg to hatch, and mother birds will lay between six and eight eggs, sometimes laying only a single egg per day, or even one egg every other day, over the course of a week.

While the mother incubates the eggs by sitting on them, the father will help by bringing food for the mother to eat. If he didn't, then the eggs would be at risk of getting too cool while the mother hunted her own food. Once the eggs hatch, the male will continue to bring food both for the mother and the chicks.

Chicks may leave the nest after about a month, and will start eating on their own after about two months, but are not considered mature until they are almost 10-months-old.

In the wild, parakeets sometimes mate for life, and in captivity they are relatively easy to breed, once a couple have successfully paired off.

LIFE SPAN

How long a parakeet lives depends largely on the type of bird that it is, as well as on the quality of its diet and care. Usually, they live for between 5 and 15 years, though some live to be as old as 20.

SIZE

The parakeet is a relatively small to medium sized parrot. Depending on the kind of bird it is, they may be as short as 7 inches, to as tall as 18 inches, when measured from the top of their head to the tip of their long tails.

HABITAT

Parakeets can be found throughout the world, in many different environments. In Australia, some types of parakeets tend to prefer the dryer, hotter interior of the continent to the wetter coastlines (though, they'll always be found near water). In contrast, in South America and Africa, they live in dense forests where it rains every day.

A few kinds of parakeets—mainly found in Australia—live and make their nests on the ground, but most live in trees.

There was only one kind of parakeet native to North America. Called the Carolina parakeet, it ranged across the east coast from New York to Florida, and inland as far as Tennessee.

The last known Carolina parakeet died in 1918. However, parakeets today can be seen throughout the United States, especially in Florida, Texas, Louisiana, and southern California. However, these kinds of birds are not native to North America. Rather, they have been brought here, often by pet owners who either let them go or lose them.

DIET

Parakeets have sharp, hooked bills that are excellent at prying open the hard outer shell of some nuts and seeds. They also eat fruits and sometimes even eat bugs and worms.

In captivity, they can eat all of these things, but also eat vegetables like zucchini, lettuce, broccoli, or carrots, as well as bird seed and special food pellets.

FRIENDS AND ENEMIES

Who is in the parakeet's neighborhood changes depending on what part of the world they're living in. In Australia, they could be found near kangaroos and wallabies and koalas. In South America, they'd be near sloths and morpho butterflies. In North America, they can be found near squirrels and opossums and other tree-dwelling animals.

Like many social, flocking birds, they can often be found mingling in trees with other kinds of birds.

No matter where they live, parakeets can fall prey to any of the major predators. Snakes, hawks, eagles, and owls are especially the parakeet's enemies, but rats too have been known to disturb their nests, as well as cats both large and small.

SUITABILITY AS PETS

Parakeets are well known to make great pets. Owners love that they can mimic speech and other sounds. Many owners will "housetrain" their birds—teaching them to use the bathroom on command in their cages—so that they can be let out to fly around a house. These birds love to interact with people, and are known for being gentle with and entertaining to children, once the child learns not to pull its feathers! They can also do well with other pets in a home—though care should be taken if that pet is a cat, dog, or snake, as they might see the bird as a quick snack!

Perhaps especially though, parakeets enjoy the company of other birds, and responsible owners should have more than a single bird in a home. Without this companionship, a parakeet may become lonely and sad, and might even start pulling out its feathers!

They are intelligent, active birds, and will play with toys and love to fly and climb from perch to perch and up and down the bars of cages.

Please leave a review for me

http://lisastrattin.com/Review-Vol-130

For more Kindle Downloads Visit Lisa Strattin Author Page on Amazon Author Central

http://amazon.com/author/lisastrattin

To see upcoming titles, visit my website at LisaStrattin.com – all books available on kindle!

http://lisastrattin.com

PLUSH PARAKEET TOY

You can get one by copying and pasting this link
into your browser:
http://lisastrattin.com/plushparakeet

KIDCRAFTS MONTHLY SUBSCRIPTION PROGRAM

Receive a Box of Crafts and a Lisa Strattin Full Color Paperback Book Each Month in Your Mailbox!

Get yours by copying and pasting this link into your browser

http://kidcraftsbylisa.com

Made in the USA
San Bernardino, CA
30 May 2019